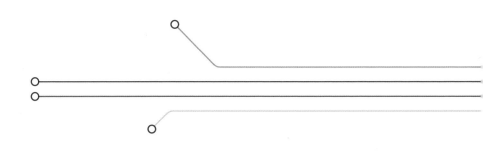

Sail On, Sail On: A Dictionary of the Sayings and Teachings of LeRoy T. Carlson, TDS Founder
Copyright © 2018 Telephone and Data Systems, Inc.
All rights reserved.
Printed in the United States of America by Suttle-Straus, Inc., Waunakee, Wisconsin.

This book is not for sale.

ISBN: 978-0-9992109-0-1

# Dedication

Roy and Margaret Carlson

Created in memory of LeRoy T. ("Roy") Carlson, founder of Telephone and Data Systems, Inc., this dictionary is dedicated to Margaret D. Carlson. She shared Roy's world and words for over seventy years as his devoted wife. Her contribution to Roy's stellar achievements and to TDS is immeasurable. We also dedicate it to all of our stakeholders, especially the past and current employees of the TDS enterprise. Their excellence and high level of commitment have made TDS into an outstanding company of which we can all be justifiably proud.

# Columbus

Joaquin Miller

BEHIND him lay the gray Azores,
Behind the Gates of Hercules;
Before him not the ghost of shores,
Before him only shoreless seas.
The good mate said: "Now must we pray,    5
For lo! the very stars are gone.
Brave Admiral, speak, what shall I say?"
"Why, say, 'Sail on! sail on! and on!'"

"My men grow mutinous day by day;
My men grow ghastly wan and weak."    10
The stout mate thought of home; a spray
Of salt wave washed his swarthy cheek.
"What shall I say, brave Admiral, say,
If we sight naught but seas at dawn?"
"Why, you shall say at break of day,    15
 'Sail on! sail on! sail on! and on!'"

They sailed and sailed, as winds might blow,
Until at last the blanched mate said:
"Why, now not even God would know
Should I and all my men fall dead.    20
These very winds forget their way,
For God from these dread seas is gone.
Now speak, brave Admiral, speak and say"—
He said: "Sail on! sail on! and on!"

They sailed. They sailed. Then spake the mate:    25
"This mad sea shows his teeth to-night.
He curls his lip, he lies in wait,
With lifted teeth, as if to bite!
Brave Admiral, say but one good word:
What shall we do when hope is gone?"    30
The words leapt like a leaping sword:
"Sail on! sail on! sail on! and on!"

Then, pale and worn, he kept his deck,
And peered through darkness. Ah, that night
Of all dark nights! And then a speck—    35
A light! A light! A light! A light!
It grew, a starlit flag unfurled!
It grew to be Time's burst of dawn.
He gained a world; he gave that world
Its grandest lesson: "On! sail on!"    40

[Edmund Clarence Stedman, ed. (1833–1908). *An American Anthology, 1787–1900*. From http://www.bartleby.com/248/798.html.]

# Introduction

On May 15, 2016, TDS joyfully celebrated LeRoy T. ("Roy") Carlson's 100th birthday with a special spoken "Thank-You Message," which Roy delivered to all associates:

*Thank you to all of you for your well wishes on my 100th birthday. As you know, TDS is near and dear to my heart. Thank you to each of you for all you are doing to serve our customers, to serve our society, and to serve our country. May God bless each of you.*

A special TDS Chicago office birthday celebration was held on May 19th. At this time Ted and Walter Carlson honored Roy with special toasts; the attendees sang *Happy Birthday*; and Roy once again "addressed the team," expressing his appreciation for all they did to make TDS successful. A card, signed by all present, heralded the "Birthday of the Century," a card that he was most pleased to receive. Four days later, on May 23rd, Roy passed away.

One of Roy's favorite poems, which he often quoted in messages to inspire team members, was "Columbus," by Joaquin Miller (*opposite page*). The poem tells the story of Christopher Columbus crossing the Atlantic to discover the New World. It illustrates the unrelenting perseverance a leader must have to accomplish a mission. Roy used it to encourage people to innovate, to seek new vistas, and to never give up.

As the poem's last stanza illustrates, Columbus' dauntless persistence was rewarded. Like Columbus, Roy was a dedicated leader who sought out the new and never gave up. He "gained a world"—the world of TDS and all that it has encompassed, including spirited colleagues in a burgeoning industry,

Roy Carlson at his desk.

# Introduction (continued)

hardworking employees and associates, caring friends, a remarkable family, and a supportive wife, who all joined him in the voyage—and Roy "gave that world its grandest lesson: 'On! sail on!'"

Roy started his business career as a young boy on Chicago's South Side, selling fruit and vegetables from a cart to help with the family's income during the Great Depression. He earned a bachelor's degree in business at the University of Chicago and an MBA from Harvard Business School. During WWII, he served his country in several important capacities. Roy then worked for two business organizations, after which he embarked on his life's work: owning and operating communications-related businesses.

Roy's experiences with these enterprises, together with his entrepreneurial mind-set and great interest in and admiration for the communications industry, led him to acquire, in 1967 and 1968, ten small, rural, independent, Wisconsin telephone companies that formed the early foundation of Telephone and Data Systems, Inc. [NYSE: TDS]. His vision, leadership, focus, and resolve, and his intense conviction that TDS be a "continuously learning company," were critical factors in TDS becoming a leading communications company.

As chairman from the company's founding in 1969 until 2002, and from then on as chairman emeritus, Roy was the company's consummate inspirer and teacher. His insatiable curiosity included a fascination with words, especially their meaning and power. Roy's colorful sayings, or "Royisms" (many original and some borrowed), have become well-known touchstones and maxims within the company. They have a strong educational and motivational focus, which is perhaps best expressed by this Royism: "We run a school as much as a business."

In celebration of Roy Carlson's incredible century of life, and to continue his commitment to inspiring and teaching, this book, *Sail On, Sail On: A Dictionary of the Sayings and Teachings of LeRoy T. Carlson, TDS Founder*, was created. It includes Royisms remembered by Roy's colleagues, employees, associates, friends, and family members.

The book is divided into three parts. The first part includes Roy's notable sayings and teachings, arranged alphabetically by keyword(s), along with illustrative stories and photos. To the left of each letter of the alphabet are some of Roy's personal attributes many of which reflect his entrepreneurial spirit.

In the second part of the book, one finds several of Roy's favorite teaching aids: the compounding articles ("Compounding: It's Boring, But a Wonder," and "Worth Effecting Steadily"); "The Man in the Chair"; "THINK" signs (which in the early years Roy gave to TDS employees); Roy's rulers; and two of his favorite poems (excerpts from "Horatius at the Bridge," by Lord Thomas Babington Macaulay, and "We Thank Thee," traditionally attributed to Ralph Waldo Emerson).

Finally, in part three are Roy's life story, celebration photos, and closing remarks.

Roy continues to be an inspiration to all of us. This dictionary provides a sample of his wisdom as an educator and as a servant leader. We hope you find it enjoyable to read, learn from, and use as a handy reference tool for yourself and your family, as you, too, serve society by "sailing on."


Ted Herbert                    Arda J. Hovnanian


*(For more information about TDS's founder, associates and employees are invited to visit Roy's TDS intranet website page at: Enterprise Point > Business Units > Corporate > Founder's Page.)*

# Part One
## Sayings and Teachings A to Z

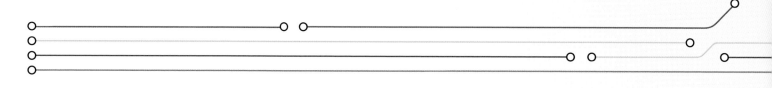

# "You don't want anything in the **ATTIC** that eats."

❝ One Friday, I met Roy at O'Hare for a two-hour meeting, fully expecting to return to Madison that evening. However, an urgent phone call regarding an acquisition required us to spend the next two days in Rochester, New York, in order to acquire a telephone company that included in its list of assets—a LION. During our visit, a group of us were having breakfast with an Arthur Andersen partner. I will never forget the bewildered look on the partner's face after he inquired about our latest acquisition, and Roy replied, 'It eats a cow, every day.' ❞

– **Arland Hocker**

# Accomplished Achiever Activist Adaptive Admirable Adventurous Ageless Ambitious Appreciative Articulate Assertive Assured Astute Authentic

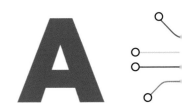

"Continuously compliment and **ACKNOWLEDGE** all levels of accomplishment."

"You may have to call on an **ACQUISITION** candidate twenty-five years or more to make the sale" (don't give up).

"**ACT**" (take action; don't just contemplate).

"You have to **ADJUST**."

"Give away your possessions while you are **ALIVE** as no one knows what will happen after you are gone."

"Honor people when they are **ALIVE** because you won't be able to do it when they are gone."

"**AMERICA** is a good place to be for people who want to work."

"**ANALYZE** it 'six ways from Sunday'" (be thorough and complete; find many ways to solve a problem).

"You don't want anything in the **ATTIC** that eats" (get rid of what is too expensive to maintain or no longer useful).

## "BUILD it in your own image."

“ Upon his return, Roy gave a few of us a brief account of his trip to Sweden. One thing in particular he told us about was an inscription on a tombstone in an ancient Nordic cemetery. A guide had translated it for Roy: '… My father's gods are not my gods.' (Most present understood that those words made an impression on Roy. Knowing Roy, the reason he gave us this account was to impart those words.)

I understood that the point of the inscription was to convey at least two things: (1) Ted would lead the company differently than Roy had. (2) When you raise your children, even as you spend considerable time and effort imparting your values and 'gods' to them, they will live their lives as best suits them, and they will be true to themselves. ”

– Bill DeCarlo

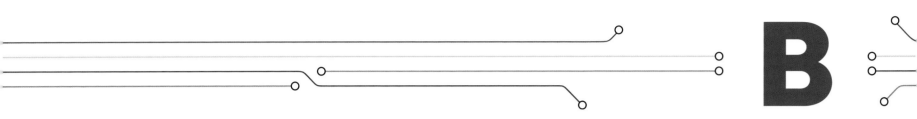

**B**

"Hold on to the **BRAKES**" (maintain power to stop something after it's begun).

"Look for ways to **BROADEN** your children's horizons."

"We must **BUILD** America."

"**BUILD** it in your own image" (build to your strengths and interests).

"**BUILD** on your accomplishments."

"It's easy to sell a business; it's hard to **BUILD** one."

"**BULL** it through" (get it done).

"Burdensome **BUREAUCRACIES** hurt the company."

"Treat your attorneys as part of your **BUSINESS** and team."

"Don't be a '**BUSINESS BUM**'" (be disciplined; set limits; have high standards and aspirations; and pace yourself for the long term).

"**BUSINESS SCHOOL** is a good path to a good business career."

"**BUY** right" (only buy something if you can get a good price and if it is useful).

"**BUYING** is selling" (the buyer needs to convince the seller to do business with him or her).

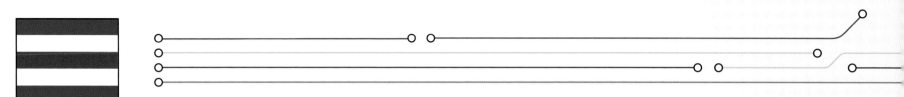

"Take **CARE** of your people."

" It was a cold, windy, and snowy night on LaSalle Street in Chicago, around 9:30 PM. ...Several of us had attended a late-evening office meeting, and we had no means to get home to Wisconsin. Roy called Margaret and asked her to drive their car from Evanston to downtown Chicago, so we could borrow it and drive it home. We obviously expected to drive them home, first, then head north. Roy graciously refused our invitation and urged us to drive carefully. Off Roy and his dear wife went, marching through the snow to the train station. We stood there in disbelief! We just couldn't believe that he AND Mrs. Carlson could be so accommodating. This act of kindness, and hundreds like it in years past, left a telling impression on us. That's all we talked about on the way home. We couldn't believe it! "

– **Charlie Ricker**

Candid Careful Caring Challenging Charismatic Coach Committed Communicator Competent Competitor Complex Confident Conscientious Convincing Courageous Creative Curious Current

"Take **CARE** of matters when there is hay in the barn because it will be a lot harder when there's none."

"Take **CARE** of your people."

"**CASH** business comes first" (when there is a purchase, sale, or matter concerning an external customer, other items can wait).

"**CASH** is king" (stay fiscally sound and have the cash on hand to make good acquisitions).

"Be **CHARITABLE**."

"**CHECK** and cross-check" (regarding numbers, assumptions, and all matters generally).

"If you have trouble making a **CHOICE**, flip a coin. If you don't like what comes up, choose the other path" (follow your instincts).

"Give your team the 'power of **CHOICE**'" (provide articles, books, and information, and let team members select what is most useful).

"Don't fight **CITY HALL**" (work with the government).

"**CLEAN** up after the party's over" (don't leave things undone).

"A manager's job is to **CLEAR** the roadblocks out of the way."

"The team must be **CLEAR-EYED**" (well-rested, alert, and ready to work).

"**CLOSE** the loop" (be complete and inform those who should know).

"Be **COMFORTABLE** with yourself."

"Honor your **COMMITMENTS**."

"If you're not 110 percent **COMMITTED**, don't do it."

"You need to have **COMMON SENSE**."

"The most important people in the **COMPANY** are the reception desk and mailroom staffers: the receptionist gives our first impression, and if the mail isn't handled in a timely manner, there is no point to our efforts."

"Choose an industry where you have the ability to **COMPETE** successfully and where you can win against the competition."

"**COMPETITION** isn't too bad as long as you've got intelligent competitors."

"Collect the facts; be **COMPLETE** and precise."

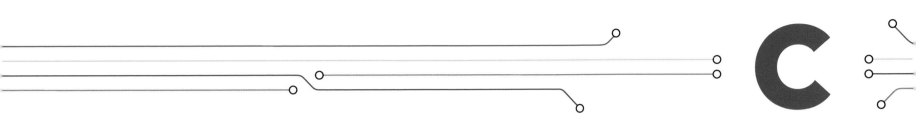

"Don't lose **CONTROL**" (of your business or of yourself).

"Work the room and work the **CONVENTION**."

"**CORRECT** a problem before it grows."

"Find your **COTERIE**, your covey."

"Have guts—**COURAGE** to do what is right and only that."

"You must be **CREATIVE**."

"Give the **CREDIT** to others."

"If it doesn't help your **CUSTOMER**, it's probably not worth doing."

"Remember who we work for: we work for our **CUSTOMERS**."

"See the world through our **CUSTOMERS**' eyes."

"Leaders, including top executives, must visit **CUSTOMERS** regularly."

"If we don't have **CUSTOMERS**, we don't have a company."

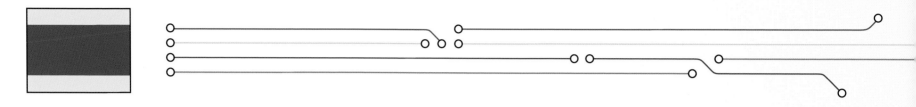

"**DO** whatever it takes
to be successful."

> Roy called a spouse to find out where
> a development team member was. She said,
> 'Somewhere on the road in Tennessee.' To
> which Roy replied, 'He has to eat lunch. Call
> the closest McDonald's and tell them to have
> him call me!'

– **Paul Forshay**

# Daring Dauntless Decisive Dedicated Dependable Determined Diligent Disciplined Dutiful Dynamic

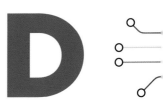

"Don't give me any **DATA** that's 'antique'" (don't give me old data).

"Don't lose a **DEAL** over 5 percent."

"**DEBT** you owe to others is hard money. Debt owed to yourself is soft money. Avoid hard money."

"Make the **DECISION** and take ownership of it."

"When there's no one there of higher authority, and a **DECISION** needs to be made, make it."

"Never make an important **DECISION** when you are tired."

"**DEFEAT** is only for those who accept it."

"Be sure they have **DESSERT**" (celebrate success).

"**DEVELOP** only that which is good and worthwhile."

"Discipline and **DILIGENCE** avail all" (these are more useful and important than anything else).

"Never say, 'I'll try to do it.' Just say, 'I'll do it.' Don't try—**DO**."

## "DRESS sharply."

TDS Chicago associates demonstrate the importance of a friendly yellow tie to a "young recruit."

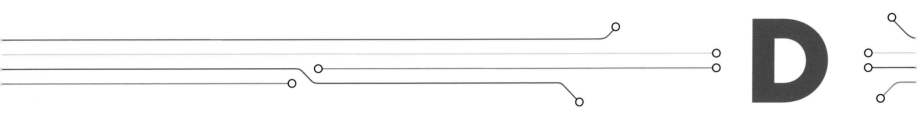

"Nothing to do, but to **DO** it."

"**DO** it now!"

"**DO** it pleasantly."

"**DO** whatever it takes to be successful."

"Says easy. **DOES** hard."

"Squeeze each **DOLLAR** twice before you spend it."

"Just get it **DONE**!"

"Don't **DOUBLE-HANDLE** anything."

"Much of the world judges by appearances, so **DRESS** sharply."

"**DRIVE** your own car."

"If it walks like a **DUCK**, it must be a **DUCK**" (see things for what they are).

"Let everyone do his or her **DUTY**."

"**DUTY** is beauty."

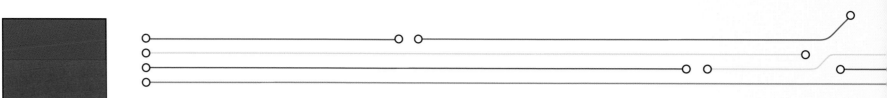

## "EDUCATE, EDUCATE, EDUCATE."

" I distinctly remember how Uncle Roy and Aunt Margaret used to mail us a big, heavy box each holiday season. When he thought he was bringing us joy, the truth was that when we received it, we would groan and say, 'Not another box of books again this Christmas!' We would ask Mom and Dad, 'When are we going to get any real presents?' Little did we know that the gift of education was one we would grow to appreciate more and more. "

– **Byron Wertz**

# Earnest Ebullient Educator Effective Empathetic Empowering Encouraging Enduring Energetic Enthusiastic Entrepreneurial Estimable Ethical Extroverted Exuberant

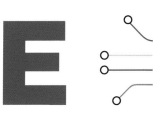

"**EARN** your pay."

"**EASE** it through" (sometimes you need a soft touch).

"If it were **EASY**, I'd do it myself."

"**EDUCATE, EDUCATE, EDUCATE.**"

"**EDUCATION** is critical" (educated employees are better equipped to serve the customer).

"**EEEEEEEASY** does it."

"Make whatever **EFFORT** is needed to make the deal" (honor prospective buyers or sellers by visiting with them on their own turf).

"Apply **ELBOW** grease" (work hard to implement your ideas).

"Each of us is like a blind person touching one part of an **ELEPHANT**" (we only comprehend the part of the situation that we encounter).

"Ducks migrating in formation **ENCOURAGE** each other by honking. 'Honk' at your team!"

"Writing makes an **EXACT** person."

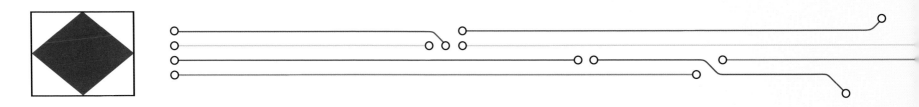

"FINISH strong."

" It was 4:30 p.m. on New Year's Eve. The office was very quiet, and we were wrapping up the January 1st insurance renewal. We were chatting in the hallway as Roy approached in his trench coat. He began to speak, as he put on his fedora. Just at the moment that we expected him to encourage us to get home for the holiday, instead, in his soft baritone voice, he advised us in no uncertain terms: 'Finish strong, gentlemen.' "

– John Toomey and Josh Harwood

# Fair Faithful Fearless Flexible Focused Forceful Friendly Frugal

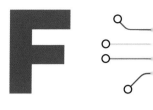

"Keep the **FAITH**."

"Have **FAITH** that you have the ability to be successful."

"If you are not with it 28 hours a day and 8 days a week, you **FALL** behind the 8-ball" (devote your time to reach your goals).

"Do what it takes to support and care for your **FAMILY**."

"God doesn't count against you the time you spend with your **FAMILY**."

"Help a person's **FAMILY** and you help them."

"Honor a person's **FAMILY** and you honor the person."

"**FATIGUE** makes cowards of us all."

"An army marches on its stomach; the generals **FEED** the troops" (care for your team and provide it with meaningful work).

"Give me all the **FIGURE FACTS**" (give me the numbers).

"**FINISH** strong" (work hard to the very end).

"Hold your feet to the **FIRE**."

"Take the **FIRST** step" (don't wait for someone to come to you).

> "An army marches on its stomach; the generals **FEED** the troops."

The "generals" and some of the "troops" from TDS Telecom, U.S. Cellular, and Suttle-Straus.

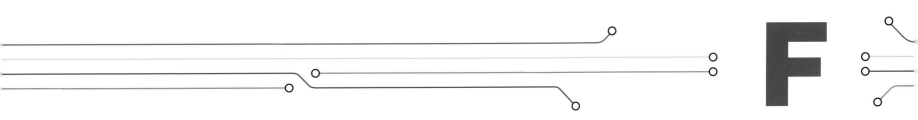

"Be **FISHY-EYED**" (be unemotional and attentive; keep your eyes open).

"You catch more **FLIES** with honey than with vinegar, and you catch more flies with the door open than with it closed."

"Be the **FLUX** (as in soldering, be the part of the team that holds the different parts of the structure together)."

"Stay **FOCUSED**."

"**FOLLOW** the other person's mind" (listen carefully to anticipate what the other person really wants—particularly useful in negotiations).

"Follow through and **FOLLOW** up."

"When you have good **FRIENDS**, you can accomplish much together."

"Maintain your **FRIENDSHIPS**."

"Don't be a boiled **FROG**" (a frog thrown into hot water will jump out, but if the water is cold, then heated gradually to boiling, the frog dies).

"Have **FUN**."

"Make the **FUR** fly."

"Build for the **FUTURE**."

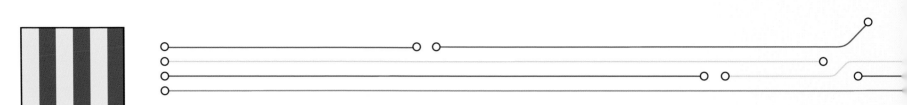

# "Read the 'GREAT BOOKS' to gain an appreciation and understanding of our world."

❝ During the twenty year period that I worked closely with Roy, I helped him research thousands of different book titles and articles, which he invariably sent to colleagues, employees, associates, friends, and family. The topics ranged widely, covering the communications industry, of course, but also general business, health, geography, history, poetry, literature, art, science, nature, and math, among others. The intention was always to help someone, and through that person, possibly help our company—and even our country.

To Roy, most questions or problems could be fixed with good research, and an article or book was immediately found to guide one to a viable solution.

Sometimes the research findings were at odds with Roy's own closely held beliefs. I asked him about this, and he replied, 'Well, so what? I just want to get 'em thinking.' Roy welcomed debate. He was not only a thinker but also a doer. He expected action to follow 'the knowledge,' once acquired.

In part, Roy's love of books came from his undergraduate days at the University of Chicago, during the 1930s, when its "Great Books" program was in its heyday. The concept that you could capture the most important ideas of western civilization, simply by identifying and reading several dozen of history's most influential books, struck a chord in Roy. I've always thought this influenced his method of pursuing and sharing knowledge, going forward. ❞

– **Arda J. Hovnanian**

# Generous Genial Gentlemanly Genuine Gifted Giving Gracious Grateful Gregarious Grounded Guide

"You have to **GET** started somewhere."

"You have to have a **GIMLET EYE**" (be sharp-sighted; observe things closely).

"Get out and **GO**" (Roy's morning message to himself).

"Look for the **GOLDEN NUGGETS** and search for the golden threads" (search for hidden value).

"Once it is **GONE**, it is gone" (regarding money, time, and other resources).

"Read the '**GREAT BOOKS**' to gain an appreciation and understanding of our world."

"Constantly evolve to **GROW**."

"We all **GROW** the company" (everyone has a responsibility to advance the company).

"**GROW** your business when the terms are favorable."

"**GROWTH** is important. Otherwise, you are dying."

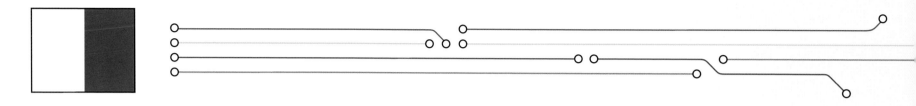

## "How can I HELP you?"

> Roy had an incredible ability to motivate. It's because he cared...about people and our business. I still remember his late Friday phone calls to make sure I received a document or a fax.... the questions he asked to make sure I listened to the conference call.... the sharing of past business mistakes and successes to help refine and shape decisions and judgments I face today.... At the close of every conversation, Roy always remembered to ask, 'How can we help?'

**– Jim Butman**

# Hale Hardworking Helpful High-minded High-powered Honest Honorable Hopeful Hospitable Humble Humorous

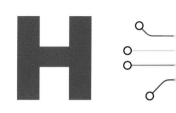

"Twenty-six repetitions make a **HABIT**."

"Develop and practice good **HABITS**, including mental habits."

"You can't get it out of your fingers unless it is first in your **HEAD**" (action must be preceded by thought).

"Preserve your **HEALTH** and your mind" (don't abuse drugs or alcohol).

"**HEALTH** first! Your health is more important than anything else."

"Maintain excellent corporate **HEALTH**, internally and externally."

"You must say something three times for it to be **HEARD**" (embrace occasional repetition to enhance learning).

"Ask others for **HELP** if you need it."

"Each morning ask your associates: 'How can I **HELP** you?'"

"If someone offers to **HELP** you, *let them*."

"Don't always be the **HIGH BIDDER**, or you will soon be on the street wearing a sandwich board."

## "Do your HOMEWORK."

Roy in class at Tilden Technical High School, Chicago (center, white shirt).

"Find out what a person's **HOBBY** is" (find common ground).

"Ask your team, 'What fat **HOG** have you slain today?'" (Inspire them to have major accomplishments each day.)

"Be there; sit in the front row; do your **HOMEWORK**; read forty pages ahead; ask questions; get tutoring, if needed" (be a good learner).

"All **HONEST** work is good work."

"You **HONOR** your co-workers when you visit them in their offices, instead of having them meet you in yours."

"Sometimes you have to show the **HORSE** the shadow of the whip" (a person may need to fear the consequences of failure to be more productive).

"You have to have a sense of **HUMOR**."

"Hire people who are **HUNGRY**" (who are strongly motivated to work hard).

"Happy **HUNTING**" (turn your work into a hunt for excellent solutions to the challenges faced each day).

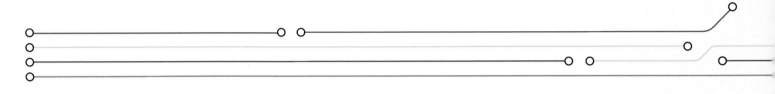

"A person with a good **IDEA**, or a new idea, is no longer the same person."

" Another important characteristic of Roy's was his very inquisitive nature. I would often see Roy sitting in industry meetings totally focused on the speakers. He searched for new directions, new ideas, and new ways of working. He continued the quest for information on exhibition floors, visiting with suppliers and seeking their new ideas to help his company achieve even better performance. His search extended to small suppliers who often had 'next generation' technology, which Roy embraced. Very few top executives commit themselves to the arduous process of seeking out, first hand, the ideas that make an important difference. He committed himself to a lifetime of learning. "

– **Bob Janowiak**

Imaginative Incisive Independent Industrious Ingenious Initiator Innovative Inquisitive Insightful Inspirational Instructive Integrator Intellectual Intuitive

"You never know who will give you a great **IDEA**."

"When you have a good **IDEA**, do it now if possible."

"A person with a good **IDEA**, or a new idea, is no longer the same person."

"Take advantage of new forms of collecting, assembling, and analyzing **IDEAS**."

"Ask your team members, 'What new **IDEAS** do you have for me today?'" (Never be complacent.)

"Write down your **IDEAS** when they come to you."

"To get what you expect, **INSPECT**."

"It's a good person who **INSPECTS** what he gets and gets what he pays for."

"**INTENSIFY** production and speed results."

"Follow your nose; appreciate and believe in your **INTUITION**" (your "sixth sense").

"**INVESTIGATE** paradoxical incidents."

"A good **INVESTMENT** will only pay off if it is operated well."

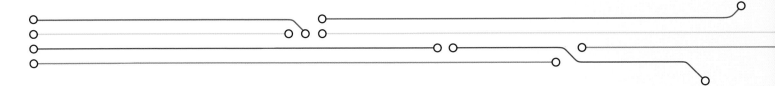

"Good **JUDGMENT** is most valuable."

In the early 1970s, we had significant regulatory issues with the Wisconsin Public Service Commission (PSC).... The life of TDS rested on getting fair and reasonable treatment from them.... Early in 1972, we received several very disappointing rulings that threatened the financial viability of our operations.... We were granted an appointment with the Director.... We researched the issues, and I presented our case with passion, but Roy quickly concluded that our pleading was going nowhere. With a kick from him in the shins under the table, I got the message to 'put a lid on it.' Roy leaned forward in his chair and said, '...Tell us what you want us to do, and we will do it, but give us the financial wherewithal to do so.' With that, we thanked the Director for his time and left.

On the way back, Roy told me that 'sometimes you just have to trust that the other guy will do the right thing.' Going forward, decisions out of the PSC improved, and Wisconsin became one of the best states in which we operated.

– **Bill Grabel**

# Jaunty Jocular Johnny-on-the-spot Jovial Judge Judicious Just

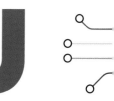

"**JOIN** me, now" (time for a meeting).

"Every company **JOINING** us brings people and assets that are shared by all."

"The longest **JOURNEY** starts with the first step."

"Good **JUDGMENT** is most valuable."

"Work with people who have good **JUDGMENT**; trust their assessments when you get them."

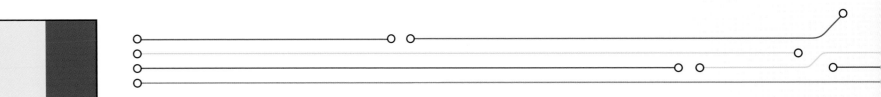

"**KNOW** your customers."

 Several times a year, representatives from throughout the organization would converge on a TDS operating company to conduct a Founder's Day celebration in which Roy would participate. We would spend the entire day visiting customers, discussing quality of services and new services, and listening to any concerns customers might have. The customers really appreciated a visit from a company representative. In several instances, we discovered major service problems, and as a result, we were able to move swiftly to correct the problems. Roy's team was always the last to return in the evening. He truly enjoyed visiting with the customers.

**– Vince Reed**

# Keen Keyman Keystone Kind Knowing Knowledgeable

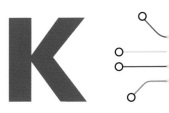

"Do it with a high **KICK**" (if you do it, do it right; be bold; be a leader; get out in front of issues).

"You have to get out of your office and **KNOCK** on doors" (you can't buy companies by sitting behind your desk).

"**KNOW** the trend lines" (know where things are going).

"**KNOW** your competitors cold" (know everything about them).

"**KNOW** your customers."

"Continue to constantly improve habits, **KNOWLEDGE**, and analysis."

"**KNOWLEDGE** is power."

"Cross-pollinate **KNOWLEDGE**" (share knowledge across job functions, and between departments, business units, parts of a diverse industry, and beyond).

"Circle the **KNOWLEDGE**" (share knowledge widely).

"**KNOWLEDGE** shared is knowledge squared."

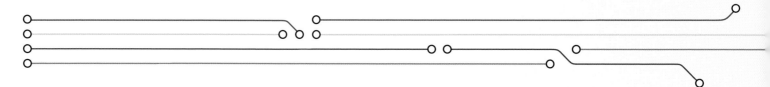

"We even pick up the **LINT** off the floor."

**"** Roy exemplified the principle that no job is too menial if the occasion calls for it. We had a distinguished visitor in our office on Monroe Street one Saturday morning. As was customary, the office coffeepot was brewing, and in fact, we even had some doughnuts. In the course of events, the visitor spilled coffee on Roy's new light gray rug. As soon as the meeting ended and the visitor departed, we rolled out a bucket of warm water, and Roy and I spent a half hour on our knees, successfully washing out the stain. **"**

– **William Vance**

Laudable Launcher Law-abiding Leader Lecturer Legendary Levelheaded Likable Listener Loyal Lucky Luminary Lutheran

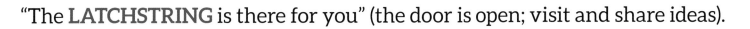

"The **LATCHSTRING** is there for you" (the door is open; visit and share ideas).

"You must be able to **LAUGH** at yourself."

"Remember the team allows us to **LEAD** them" (you need the "consent of the governed" to be successful).

"The symphony **LEADER'S** function is to focus the orchestra on their responsibilities and opportunities."

"Take less experienced team members to meetings to help them **LEARN**."

"You **LEARN** by hearing, and you **LEARN** by doing."

"**LEARN** from your mistakes."

"Some people **LEARN** more than they are taught."

"The only way to really **LEARN** something is to teach it to someone else."

"**LEARNING** is a lifelong journey."

"You can be **LEGISLATED** or regulated into business and **LEGISLATED** or regulated out of business."

"A sailmaker
uses a **LOFT**."

“ I remember putting together our first balance sheet
and income statement on a seven-column worksheet. (Our
first income statement showed the grand total earnings of
three cents per share.) Jokingly, I said I was running out of
columns on my worksheet, because Roy and K.C. August
were acquiring so many companies so fast. (At one stretch, we
acquired eight telephone companies in eight months.) Roy's
reply was, 'Arland, a sailmaker uses a loft.' ”

– **Arland Hocker**

"Make **LEMONADE** out of lemons" (make positives out of negatives).

"Keep **LETTERS** and memos 'staccato'—short and to the point."

"When you have **LEVERAGE,** use it."

"**LIFE** is sweet."

"We even pick up the **LINT** off the floor" (in reaching your goal, no detail is unimportant or task too menial).

"**LISTEN** to good advice."

"**LOANS** and debts have to be repaid."

"A sailmaker uses a **LOFT**" (plan ahead and create space in which to grow).

"It gets **LONELY** on the road" (keep your team's spirits up, because buying companies is not easy work).

"Don't **LOSE** the deal over small issues."

"If you **LOVE** what you do, it isn't work."

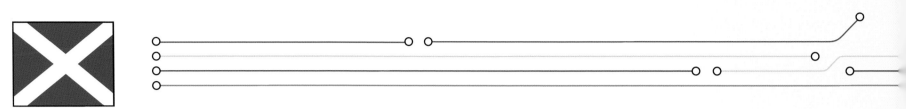

# "Look at yourself in the MIRROR."

" Roy told the story of the opportunity he had to purchase a telephone company in Mexico's Baja Peninsula. He made a few trips to visit the owner and size up the opportunity, which appeared good. Roy was close to agreeing to buy the company. When getting dressed at his hotel the morning of his final visit, Roy looked at himself in the mirror. This caused him to ask himself: 'Do you speak Spanish? Do you understand the customs and culture? Are you prepared to live here, and move, and raise your family here?' The answers to all of the questions were no, and so Roy did not buy the company. The lessons from this story are not to take on something unless you are fully committed to it, and not to take on something that you don't understand or aren't prepared to make a full effort to understand. "

– Bill DeCarlo

# Managerial Masterful Memorable Meritorious Meticulous Mindful Modest Motivated

"Never add what cannot be properly **MANAGED**."

"Companies fail when the **MARKET** moves away from the company, or when the company moves away from the market."

"The business purpose must follow the **MARKET** 'nose'" (keep up with changing market conditions).

"Ask yourself, 'What does it **MEAN**? What does it **MEAN**? What does it **MEAN**?'"

"**MEASURE** twice and cut once" (be careful when planning).

"Travel to your **MEETING** the night before" (don't take the chance of not getting the job done).

"Feed your **MIND**."

"Use your connective and creative **MIND**" (bring all your experience, knowledge, and imagination to bear).

"Three people's **MINDS** are better than one, and seven are better than three."

"Look at yourself in the **MIRROR** before you make an important decision" (consider it carefully).

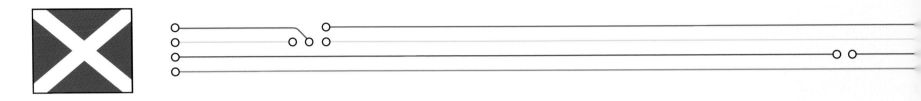

"My best sayings
are from my **MOTHER**."

Gerda Marie Swanson Carlson, Roy's mother.

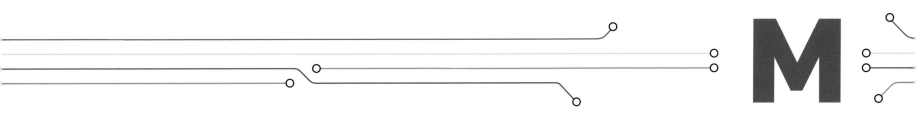

"Adopt a pretzel-like stance to accomplish the **MISSION**" (be prepared to change direction, if necessary).

"If you correct a **MISTAKE**, you haven't made it."

"People who make **MONEY** with you will rarely, if ever, sue you."

"**MONOPOLY** is a great game to play with youngsters; it develops their entrepreneurial spirit."

"You can't get better than '**MOST**'" (tell someone they are "most helpful" or their work is "most important").

"My best sayings are from my **MOTHER**."

"**MOVE** it along."

"Nothing **MOVES** by itself" (you must make things happen).

"I don't ask more of others than I have asked of **MYSELF**."

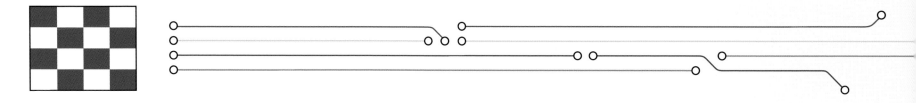

## "NEVER give up."

" While there has never been a shortage of stories, parables, and sometimes outright riddles, Roy's teaching has been mainly by example. Work harder and longer, but smarter, than the other fellow. Never give up. I can't count the number of times when the rest of the team thought a deal was dead or lost; Roy refused to accept what seemed obvious to the rest of us, and 'Roy's will' usually prevailed. It was almost eerie at times, but also inspirational, how his tenacity was rewarded. "

– Steve Fitzell

# Navigator Negotiator Neighborly Nimble Noble Nonconformist No-nonsense Nonpareil Nonstop Notable Nurturing

"Do what's **NECESSARY** until you get 'blue in the face,' and after you get blue, don't stop until you get purple!"

"Find a **NEED** and fill it."

"**NET PROFIT**, after full treatment for federal, state, and local taxes, is what matters."

"**NEVER** give up."

"Search for the **NEW**, as you run the old; and while building the **NEW**, keep what you have strong."

"We need to find **NEW SALIENTS**" (new ideas/products/services to keep the company growing).

"Give me the bad **NEWS**, first" (be frank).

"Don't **NICKEL-AND-DIME** it" (focus on the big picture).

"**NOBLESSE OBLIGE**" (those who are privileged have a duty to help others less fortunate).

"Take copious **NOTES** and share them with the team."

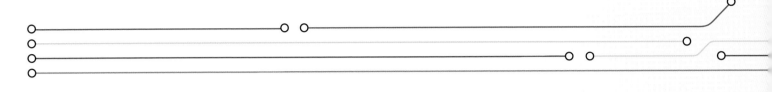

# "Focus on the next OBJECTIVE."

**"** During the 1980s and much of the 1990s, I had ample opportunity to observe Roy operate as a strategist and entrepreneur. I was struck by his ability to focus on the next objective, the next thing that needed to be done, as he phrased it, 'the next 40 miles of track.' Roy not only understood his company's strategic objectives but also its resources. He perceived, perhaps better than any business person I have ever encountered, the necessity of striving to attain one's objectives while keeping the company's resources firmly in mind. Thus, U. S. Cellular Corporation's growth, while motivated by the visionary belief that a small Midwestern telephone holding company would grow into one of the nation's premier wireless carriers, took place within a framework of caution and realism. **"**

**– Peter Connolly**

# Objective Observant Open-minded Optimistic Orator Orchestrator Original Outgoing Outspoken

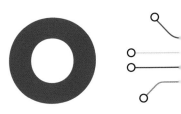

"Eat **OATMEAL** every morning and snack on walnuts" (be healthy).

"Focus on the next **OBJECTIVE**."

"You need a steel will and a velvet glove to accomplish your **OBJECTIVES**."

"Replace the **OLD** with the new" (keep your knowledge up-to-date).

"**OMISSION** can be as substantial a sin as commission" (leaving things out misleads others as much as false assertions do).

"**OPERATIONAL** success is two-thirds growing sales and one-third managing costs."

"See the world in new ways, which may be the **OPPOSITE** of how you would like to see it."

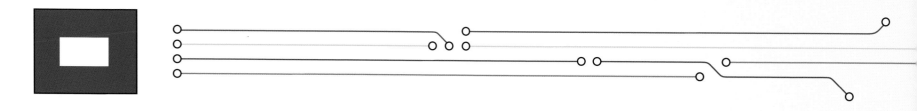

"A company
must have a
social **PURPOSE**."

❝ Who could have imagined the myriad of
wonderful consequences of securing a dependable
paycheck for ten thousand–plus families, or of
ensuring reliable communications for the thousands
of medical emergencies in the small towns served
by TDS, or of making possible the call on Christmas
morning from a soldier far from home? ❞

– **Mark Kington**

Painstaking Passionate Patient Perceptive Perfectionist Persistent Pertinent Philanthropic Positive Pragmatic Prepared Proactive Probing Progressive Proud

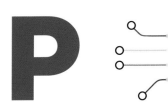

"You have to have **PATIENCE** when you develop things. You have to have steadiness. You have to stay with it."

"Be **PATIENT** with your impatience."

"**PEEL** one potato at a time" (focus on one thing at a time).

"We must control the **PEN**" (our company should draft written agreements).

"Be pleasantly **PERSISTENT**."

"A place for everything and everything in its **PLACE**" (be organized).

"You get what you **PLAN**."

"Work your **PLAN**" (execute it).

"Think, **PLAN**, re-plan, and act."

"**PLANT** seeds that will grow in future springs."

"You have got to **PLOW** it, so you can reap the harvest."

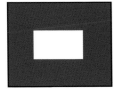
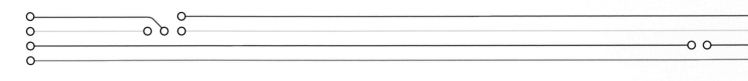

"Keep your hand on the **PLOW**" (stay the course).

"**POINT-COUNTERPOINT, POINT-COUNTERPOINT**" (push back when useful, and expect pushback).

"There are no **POLITICS** in this company" (don't play 'office politics' or encourage those who do).

"Don't '**POOR BOY**' it" (don't give anything less than your full effort; don't skimp on something important).

"Build where the **POPULATION** growth is. It will buoy up future sales results."

"Emphasize the **POSITIVE**" (as the song goes, "accentuate the positive; eliminate the negative; don't mess with Mister In-between").

"Work with 'the **POWER**'" (work with the decision-makers).

"Be **PRACTICAL** in whatever you do."

"Say a **PRAYER** before meals" (be grateful for what you have).

"Be **PRECISE**."

"**PREPARE** thoroughly before negotiating."

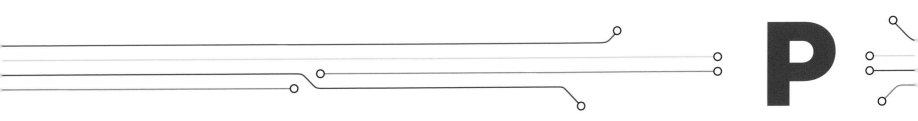

"Take a break if you are under too much **PRESSURE**. You will come back with new ideas."

"Let your subconscious mind work on a **PROBLEM**, and it will help you solve it."

"It's not enough to point to a **PROBLEM**—find the solutions."

"Reconfigure old **PROCEDURES**."

"**PRODUCE** or get changed out."

"**PROTECT** proprietary information" (don't leak to competitors).

"**PROVE** it in" (test your idea or plan).

"Be **PRUDENT** in your investments."

"**PRUNE** it. Prune the branches to make a strong tree" (prune your ideas, your finances, your time, etc.)

"**PUNCH** it up" (put it on the calendar).

"A company must have a social **PURPOSE**" (a purpose that relates to doing something important for its customers and for society, and that goes beyond purely "making money").

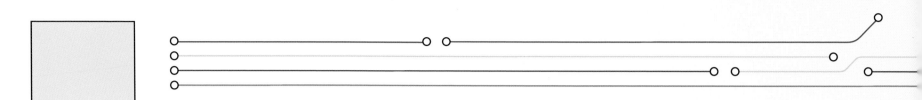

# "Ask the right QUESTIONS."

**"** Jim Barr and his team spent a couple of weeks developing a lengthy, detailed presentation for Roy, in order to justify a dollar amount that TDS Telecom would be willing to spend to acquire an attractive telephone company.

Just as Jim began to review the prepared materials, Roy asked him to stop, and instead he proceeded to ask him four or five questions. After writing down Jim's answers to each one and thinking for a minute, Roy stated what he thought the company was worth. It was exactly the same number as Jim and his team had arrived at after weeks of thought and analysis. **"**

— **Ted Herbert**

# Qualified Quality-minded Quantifier Quarterback Querier Quick-thinking Quick-witted Quotable

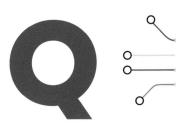

"Everyone on the team must have the highest **QUALIFICATIONS** possible."

"Do a **QUALITY** job, each day."

"**QUALITY** service comes first."

"Loyalty is the first **QUALITY** to look for in hiring."

"Ask the right **QUESTIONS**."

"Ask **QUESTIONS**" (never leave a conversation with decision-makers without getting the information you are seeking).

"If you don't work hard and act **QUICKLY**, you end up with the hindermost."

"Send inspiring **QUOTATIONS** from great thinkers to your team each morning."

## "READ at least three newspapers a day."

" So how do you get vision? I read three newspapers a day: *The New York Times, The Wall Street Journal,* and *Chicago Tribune.* I'm a member of several telephone and communications associations. I read maybe two of those publications a day at home. I get 16 other publications. I browse them and occasionally run across an article. I even include things like *Vogue.* But you have to keep-up on your function as well as your vision. Now it's darn hard to go out and read all this stuff, get it in your mind, assimilate it, and still do a full day's work at your regular job. But to survive, you have to do it.

There's the old ax story. These two fellas were in a contest, and they had so many hours to chop trees down. So one fella worked at it all the time, and the other fella took a break, every so often. And, at the end of the day, they compared how much wood they chopped. And they found the fella who had taken periodic breaks actually had chopped more wood. So the question was, 'How could he have produced more?' And the answer was, 'During his breaks, he sharpened his ax!' So we learn that we all have to sharpen our tools and then continue.

We get, maybe, fifteen to eighteen analyst reports on different parts of the industry on a regular basis, and, of course, I browse them. Now that's how you get vision. So, vision is composed of reading, studying, comparing, doing, and acting on the knowledge we have. "

**– Roy Carlson's speech at "TDS Telecom's 1999 Leadership Conference"**

# Reasonable Reliable Religious Remarkable Resilient Resourceful Respected Responsible Righteous Risk-taker

"**READ** at least three newspapers a day" (keep informed).

"**READ** business biographies."

"**REALIZE** what you have when you have it."

"Never let go of the **REINS**."

"Your **REPUTATION** is priceless."

"List the **RESOURCES** you will need before you begin a venture."

"Tie a **RIBBON** on it" (get it done with a flourish).

"Do it **RIGHT** and learn it **RIGHT** the first time, so you don't have to redo or re-learn it later on, which is much harder."

"Do the **RIGHT** thing."

"**RIPEN** by degrees" (gradually win people over to new ideas).

"**ROW** in the same direction" (teamwork is needed to reach the objective).

"Find someone to **RUN** with" (have a lifetime partner).

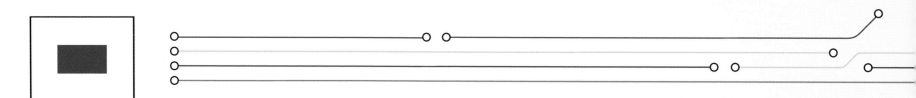

"We are all part of
the **SALES** team."

**"** In addressing the full team of employees,
Roy would request that 'all the sales team
members stand.' When only the sales folks rose
to their feet, he would make everyone stand—
accountants, engineers, technical and customer
service folks, etc., to remind us that we were all
part of the 'sales team.' **"**

– **Bill Grabel**

Sagacious Self-confident Self-disciplined Self-reliant Self-starter Sincere Skillful Smart Solid Sophisticated Spirited Steadfast Stimulating Strategic Strong Successful Supportive

**S**

"When you have made a **SALE**, hang up the phone."

"We are all part of the **SALES** team."

"We run a **SCHOOL** as much as a business" (keep learning and remain up-to-date).

"Make sure your children go to the best **SCHOOLS** possible."

"**SEARCH** for information continuously, aggressively, and ahead of competitors."

"**SEEK** and ye shall find" (favorite quotation from the Bible).

"You can't **SELL** from an empty shelf or an empty wagon."

"Be of **SERVICE**."

"Lead and close with **SERVICE**."

"**SHARE** information and **SHARE** success."

"Have evening meals with your family to **SHARE** thoughts."

"Collect your ideas in a **SHOEBOX**."

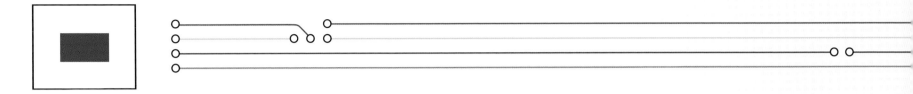

# "SMART leaders surround themselves with smart people."

Depicted above are a few teams Roy worked closely with—Top: TDS Board (2003). Bottom: Development Teams from the mid-1990s and early 1970s.

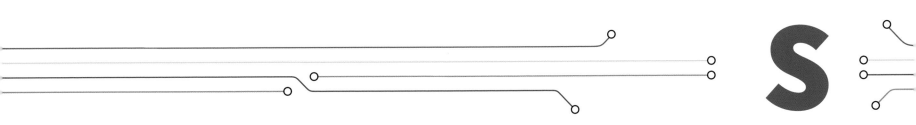

"You must make it **SINGGGGG**" (achieve clear harmony in your actions).

"You have to have 'a good **SITTER**'" (ability to sit still and concentrate in a long meeting).

"Get your **SLEEP**, but if you can't sleep, then rest; it's almost as good as sleep."

"**SMART** leaders surround themselves with smart people."

"Answer the phone with a **SMILE**."

"If you hoot with the owls, you can't **SOAR** with the eagles" (go to bed early).

"Use today's super **SOLUTIONS** for today's opportunities and needs."

"We **SPEAK** up and out" (good ideas must be heard by others).

"Recognize when you need to be the point of the **SPEAR**."

"Use due deliberate **SPEED**."

"When things **SPEED UP**, it's time to slow down" (take time to think).

"Pay attention to professional **SPORTS** to see what they can teach you about business."

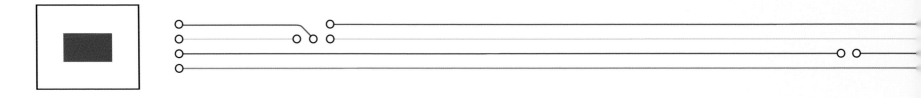

# "Collect your ideas in a SHOEBOX."

**"** ...When we first met Roy in a conference room on Segoe Road, he said that we, as auditors, needed to look hard to make sure the books of the companies TDS Telecom managed were accurate and fairly reflected the operations.

But as important as that was, we had another role. He went on to say that as a group of young auditors, we were sure to have many good ideas on improvements that could be made to the way things were done at TDS.

Roy placed a shoebox in the middle of our worktable and said that before our work was finished, the shoebox needed to be full of suggestions for improvements to the company. (Each week, we were to take one of those papers out of the box, and do it.) Then, he turned and left the room.

He probably had no idea of the impact this brief conversation would have on at least one member of this young group of auditors. I will always be looking for that one more suggestion to add to Roy's shoebox. **"**

– **Kevin Hess**

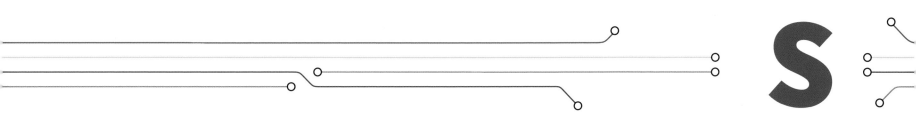

"Focus on the mackerels and don't worry about the **SPRATS**" (focus on the important things, not the inconsequential ones).

"Be **SQUARE**" (honest and dependable).

"**STAND** up for yourself."

"**STEADY ON**" (stay calm and move forward, without being rash).

"If you see me about to go through a red light, tell me to **STOP**" (don't let me make a bad decision).

"**STUDY** it to a 'fare-thee-well,' read like mad, compare."

"Nurture and care for the company's Michael Jordans—care for your **SUPERSTARS**."

"**SUSTAINABLE** improvements. Sustainable. Remember that."

"Seek to create **SWEAT EQUITY**" (create value from originality and hard work).

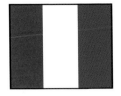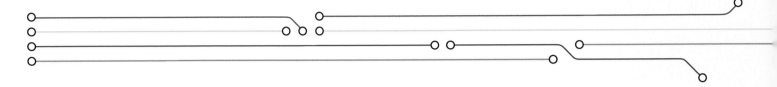

"Stay close to your **TEAM**."

**"** As many who worked for Roy Carlson could testify, one of his favorite techniques to motivate his team was the random, unexpected, personal, telephone call. He made these calls late at night, in the early morning hours, Saturdays, Sundays, holidays—whenever a thought came to his mind. Carlson used these telephone calls to instill that burst of extra effort in a particular individual at the precise moment it was needed most. Not infrequently, a call may have left an irate spouse in its wake. But, on balance, the calls had their desired effect by conveying his intense personal interest in whatever the task was. **"**

– K.C. August

# Talented Teammate Tenacious Thankful Thorough Thoughtful Thrifty Tireless Trustworthy

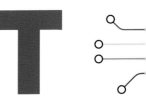

"**TALK** directly to the top person" (avoid excessive procedures and red tape, and meet with the decision-maker).

"A **TASK** may have many twists and turns before it gets done" (don't give up if negative things occur along the way).

"We need to **TEACH** and be taught."

"Stay close to your **TEAM**."

"Keep encouraging the **TEAM**, and they will keep the company going."

"Have the best **TECHNOLOGY** and best supplies to accomplish your job."

"Have two **TELEPHONE** lines, so you never miss a call."

"You have to **TELL** someone three times to have it stick in his or her head."

"*TEMPUS FUGIT*" (time flies, so "get on with it").

"We are **THANKFUL**."

"**THINK** it, then do it—think ahead."

"**THINK**" (Roy put "THINK" signs on every employee's desk at the TDS Chicago corporate office for several decades; see part two of this book).

"**THINK** with motivation, persistence, and intensity."

"Adjust constantly to improve knowledge and **THOUGHT**."

"**TIE** it down" (put it in writing and get it done).

"It takes seven **TIGERS** to bring down an elephant" (have enough resources to get a big job done).

"**TIGHTEN UP**" (collect your thoughts into a logical, practical course of action and run a "tight ship").

"**TIME** is of the essence. Be on time."

"Don't leave to tomorrow what you can do **TODAY**."

"Make a **TO-DO** list each morning and create a 'tickler file' for regular follow-up."

"Keep every **TOOL** in your toolbox sharp" (improve your skills and yourself).

"When you have a **TOUGH** problem, roll up your sleeves and get to work."

"When the going gets **TOUGH**, the tough get going."

"Map the next forty miles of **TRACK**" (maintain a vision for the future).

"**TRAIN**, influence, and improve each other."

"**TRAVEL** coach" (be frugal).

"Let no **TRIFLE** escape efficiency and organization."

"We all eat from the same **TROUGH**" (we share limited resources, so adjust and work together in harmony; serving the customer is our common goal).

"**TRUST** a person until he or she proves unworthy of it."

"Those who can't be **TRUSTED** in little things can't be trusted."

"Every religion teaches important **TRUTHS**."

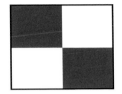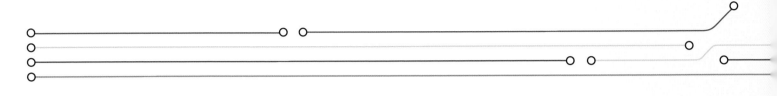

"The **UNITED STATES NAVY** was a good place through which to serve the country."

LeRoy T. Carlson, U. S. Navy, 1945.

# Unblinking Understanding Unifier Unique Unorthodox Untiring Unwavering Upholder Uplifting Upright Utilizer

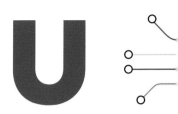

"Never **UNDERESTIMATE** the long shadow cast by the farmer" (the boss may be watching you).

"Never buy a business you—and your team—don't **UNDERSTAND** and don't know how to run."

"**UNDERSTAND** the short-term, medium-term, and long-term implications of your actions."

"**UNDERSTAND** what your team is doing and whether or not they need to do it."

"Maintain a good **UNDERSTANDING** of society and people."

"Some people have a **UNIQUE** cast of mind, and their ideas can be most helpful."

"The **UNITED STATES NAVY** was a good place through which to serve the country."

"**USE** 'please' and 'thank you' in company correspondences."

"Be **USEFUL**, and you will be valuable."

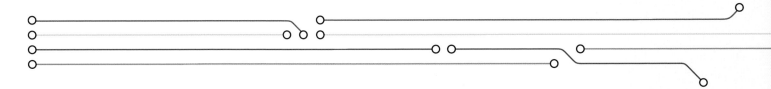

## "Have forward VISION."

"'One party' service is taken for granted today. In the 1970s...the Wisconsin State Public Commission thought it was too expensive to build, and 'party line' service in rural areas was just fine. Roy had other ideas. He had an intuitive sense... some thought he was nuts or just plain pushy... that the added cost of 'all one party' service would...benefit everyone... Roy was years ahead in his understanding...

Roy's 'sixth sense' for what people really needed and wanted for communications services served the company well...

Beginning in the early '70s...TDS started deploying IMTS mobile phone and eventually paging service. While these services were less than stellar financial activities, they served as the kindling that set the cellular bonfire at TDS."

**– Charlie Ricker**

# Valiant Validator Venturer Versatile Veteran Vibrant Vintage Visionary

"People want to stop working when they retire. They go on **VACATION** for a few months, then realize they have nothing to do" (continuing to contribute and staying engaged keeps you alert and promotes a longer, healthier life, and it also helps the team).

"Cowards die many times before their deaths; the **VALIANT** never taste of death, but once" (favorite quotation from Shakespeare's *Julius Caesar*).

"One's books and files are most **VALUABLE**."

"Create new **VALUE** by finding new niches."

"Get the best **VALUE** for your money."

"Eat your **VEGETABLES**."

"Beware of tunnel **VISION**."

"Have forward **VISION**."

"Have *many* chairs in your office for **VISITORS**."

"Keep your office door open and welcome **VISITORS**."

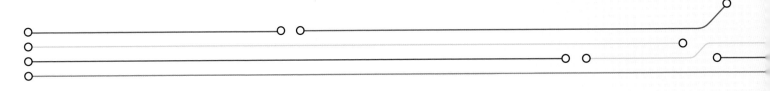

"Seek **WIN-WIN** solutions."

" A good example of Roy's 'win-win' approach with decision makers was the time he assembled his troops in Washington, in order to personally meet with a number of Senators and Representatives. He wanted to tell them that preserving the funding for the REA telephone loan programs benefited the rural Telcos through advantageous loans (a win), while also benefiting rural customers (their constituents) with modernization (a win), and cheaper phone rates (a win). "

– Bob Collins

# Warmhearted Watchful Willing Winner Wise Witty Workhorse Worthy Writer

"**WALK** around the block twice" (at brainstorming meetings, give everyone at least two opportunities to share his or her views).

"**WALK** in other people's shoes" (consider how decisions affect those involved).

"**WALK** over a mile each day" (stay in shape).

"**WALK** the office" ('manage by walking around').

"If you read *THE WALL STREET JOURNAL* every day for ten years, it's the equivalent of an MBA education."

"**WEAVE** everyone in" (include your team in decision making).

"Be the facilitator, mentor, innovator, broker, director—**WHATEVER** is needed."

"Improve everything. Even if that improvement is only 1 percent, perhaps that's all you need to **WIN**."

"It's only fun when you **WIN**."

"Seek **WIN-WIN** solutions."

"The **WINDS** blow gustily at the bow of the ship" (stay the course in the face of stress and adversity).

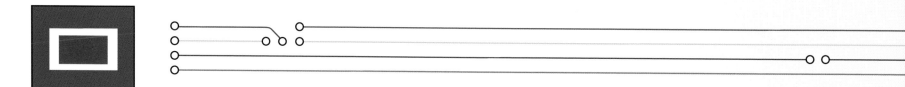

"Most people think that headquarters runs the show, but headquarters is actually controlled by the **WORK** the troops do in the field."

Top: U.S. Cellular, call center. Bottom: TDS Telecom, Network Operations training session; Suttle-Straus, sheetfed press load turner.

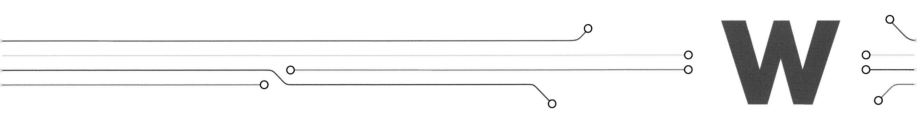

"Your **WORD** is your bond."

"Consider every single **WORD** you write. Words have meaning, impact, and power. Parse each word."

"Develop a love of **WORDS** and increase your vocabulary."

"Put in a full day's **WORK**."

"**WORK** hard."

"When you **WORK** hard, you deserve a good dinner."

"**WORK** it down" (get below the surface to understand and ensure the details are correct).

"**WORK** on weekends whenever necessary."

"Most people think that headquarters runs the show, but headquarters is actually controlled by the **WORK** the troops do in the field."

"**WORKING** hard or for a long time on something doesn't necessarily make it a good thing to do."

"**WRITE** it down, so it sticks in your head."

"**WRITE** out your talking points ahead of time and put them in your pocket."

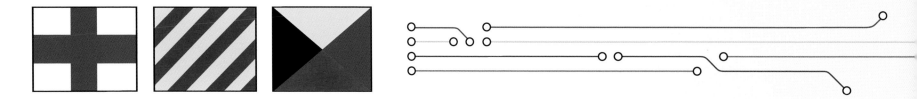

"We don't want
'YES FOLKS'
on the team."

❝ Roy felt his productive day hadn't begun until he came into the 'war room.' He really relished the competition of the M&A activities we pursued while in there.

He truly wanted those around him to be creative and tell him what they thought—no 'yes folks.' Roy was genuinely so comfortable in his skin that he sought out opposing viewpoints. ❞

– Ed Towers

X-factor  Yare  Yarn Spinner
Young at heart  Youthful
Zealous  Zestful

"At every meeting, be sure everyone has two sharp pencils and a
**YELLOW LEGAL PAD** at his or her chair."

"Keep a **YELLOW LEGAL PAD** by your bed at night" (write down ideas that
come to you in your sleep to consider the next day).

"Don't say '**YES**' without full exploration."

"We don't want '**YES FOLKS**' on the team."

"Give the '**YOUNG BUCKS**' a chance" (nurture new talent).

"Understand the world—from A to izzard, from Accounting to **ZOOLOGY**."

# Part Two
## Teaching Aids

# Compounding: It's Boring, But A Wonder

*YOUR MONEY MATTERS*
by Robert L. Rose, Staff Reporter of the Wall Street Journal
June 17, 1985

John Maynard Keynes supposedly called it magic. One of the Rothschilds is said to have proclaimed it the eighth wonder of the world. Today, people continue to extol its wonder and its glory.

The object of their affection: compound-interest, a subject that bores or confuses as many people as it impresses.

Yet understanding compound-interest can help people calculate the return on savings and investments, as well as the cost of borrowing. These calculations apply to almost any financial decision, from the reinvestment of dividends to the purchase of a zero-coupon bond for an individual retirement account.

Simply stated, compound-interest is "interest on interest." Interest earned after a given period, for example, a year, is added to the principal amount and included in the next period's interest calculation.

"With all of the time you spend working, saving, borrowing and investing," says Richard P. Brief, a New York University business professor, "one could argue that the calculations (of compound-interest) ought to be understood by most people. And it is within reach of most people.

The power of compound-interest has intrigued people for years. Early in the last century, an English astronomer, Francis Bally, figured that a British penny invested at an annual compound-interest of 5% at the birth of Christ would have yielded enough gold by 1810 to fill 357 million earths. Benjamin Franklin was more practical. At his death in 1790, he left 1,000 pounds each to the cities of Boston and Philadelphia on the condition they wouldn't touch the money for 100 years. Boston's bequest, which was equivalent to $4,500, ballooned to $332,000 by 1890.

But savers and investors don't have to live to 100 to reap its benefits.

Consider an investment with a current value of $10,000, earning an annual interest of 8%. After a year, the investment grows to $10,800 (1.08 times 10,000). After the second year, it's worth $11,664 (1.08 times $10,800). After three more years, the investment grows to $14,693.

The same concept applies to consumer borrowing. A $10,000 loan, with an 8% interest charge compounded annually, would cost $14,693 to repay in a lump sum after five years.

More frequent compounding also results in higher annual yields. For instance, if an 8% annual interest rate is compounded quarterly, the principal would grow by 2% compounded every three months. Using the earlier example, the $10,000 investment that grew to $14,693 after five years of annual compounding would grow to $14,859 with quarterly compounding. Monthly compounding would give $14,898 and weekly compounding would result in $14,914. This helps explain why, for example, one bank can offer a savings product with a higher normal interest rate than the competition, but a lower effective annual yield. It simply compounds less frequently.

Computers and calculators with built-in formulas make solving compound-interest problems relatively easy. Calculators without

---

### Figuring the Return

The formula for annual compound interest is $P \times (1+r)^n$. $P$ is the principal, $r$ is the interest rate and $n$ is the number of years.

Here are the values of $10,000 invested at 8% or 12% over various periods:

| YEARS | 8% | 12% |
|---|---|---|
| 5 | $14,693 | $17,623 |
| 10 | 21,589 | 31,058 |
| 20 | 46,610 | 96,463 |
| 40 | 217,245 | 930,510 |
| 100 | 21,997,613 | 835,222,660 |

---

the built-in formula ought to have an exponent key (see table). People can also use compound-interest tables, which, along with explanations of interest rate calculations, can be found in a free booklet published by Federal Reserve Bank of New York's public information department, 33 Liberty Street, New York, NY 10045.

Investors and savers can also take a rule-of-thumb shortcut to determine how long it would take to double a sum of money at a given interest rate with annual compounding: Divide 72 by the rate. For example, the $10,000 investment yielding 8% would double in about nine years (72 divided by 8).

But people should be aware that inflation compounds, too. Unless inflation disappears, that $20,000 investment nine years from now will be worth something less than that in today's dollars. And unless it is tax-free, the investment would be eroded further by taxes.

# Worth Effecting Steadily

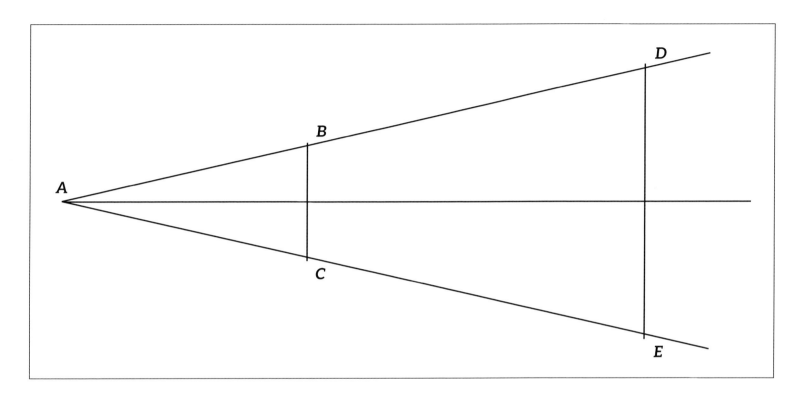

We are today at Point **"A"**. If you switch into stronger or new products now, you pay no price penalty, for many attractive products are in the same range as products with poor prospects.

**BUT**...if you postpone action and decide to switch later, say, six months from now – your products may be at Point **"C"**, or even at Point **"E"**. The products you might have developed or produced may then be at Point **"B"** or **"D"**.

The gap between **"B"** and **"C",** and the gap between **"D"** and **"E",** represents the loss you will take by failing to switch into better products now. The difference could be substantial.

You can substitute the word "common stock," or the word "procedures," or the word "habits," or other key asset items, for the word "products" above. Then by rereading, putting in the new word, you will realize the great value of the above graph. Play around with these thoughts. If your findings reveal that your position with respect to any of these asset items is not the very best position to be in at this time, then adjust your position now—not later.

# The Man in the Chair

"*I don't know who you are.*

*I don't know your company.*

*I don't know your company's product.*

*I don't know what your company stands for.*

*I don't know your company's customers.*

*I don't know your company's record.*

*I don't know your company's reputation.*

*Now–what was it you wanted to sell me?"*

**MORAL:** Sales start **before** your salesman calls–
with business publication advertising.

## McGRAW-HILL MAGAZINES
BUSINESS • PROFESSIONAL • TECHNICAL

Roy had a magazine clipping of McGraw-Hill's "The Man in the Chair" advertisement taped to his office wall for many years.

# "Think" Signs and Roy's Rulers

| THINK | DENK | ملّيًا فكّر |
|:-:|:-:|:-:|
| English | German | Arabic |

| よく考えて | 想一想 | 생각하라 |
|:-:|:-:|:-:|
| Japanese | Chinese (simplified) | Korean |

| PENSE | PIENSA |
|:-:|:-:|
| French | Spanish |

In the early days, "Think" signs, made famous by IBM, were placed at every employee's desk at the TDS Chicago corporate office. We have translated it here in different languages to represent the global nature of the communications industry.

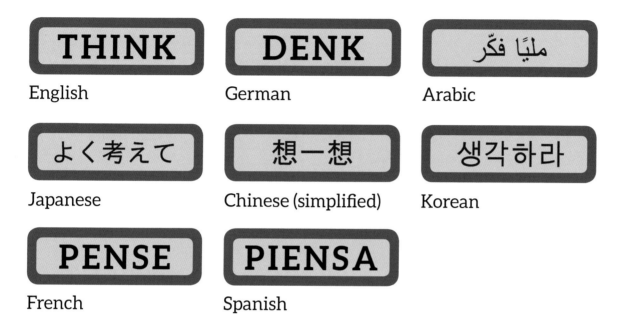

These rulers were personally designed by Roy Carlson, with the help of Suttle-Straus, and were distributed to all employees, enterprise-wide, along with our publication, the *Innovator*, which commemorated Roy's 90th birthday in 2006.

# Excerpts from "Horatius at the Bridge"

[This nineteenth-century ballad, describing a circa 500 BC battle, recounts the story of a heroic leader, Horatius, who successfully defends the City of Rome against a much larger Etruscan force. Fellow Romans join with Horatius in the battle, enabling the remaining Roman troops to dismantle the bridge across the Tiber River, and prevent the Etruscans from crossing it into Rome. The bridge collapses as the Romans retreat to safety, leaving Horatius to fight on alone. Wounded, he leaps into the river and survives the ordeal.]

**By Lord Thomas Babington Macaulay**

LARS PORSENA of Clusium,
  By the Nine Gods he swore
That the great house of Tarquin
  Should suffer wrong no more.
By the Nine Gods he swore it,    5
  And named a trysting-day,
And bade his messengers ride forth,
East and west and south and north,
  To summon his array.

East and west and south and north    10
  The messengers ride fast,
And tower and town and cottage
  Have heard the trumpet's blast.
Shame on the false Etruscan
  Who lingers in his home,    15
When Porsena of Clusium
  Is on the march for Rome!
      *   *   *

I wis[1], in all the Senate
  There was no heart so bold
But sore it ached, and fast it beat,    140
  When that ill news was told.
Forthwith up rose the Consul,
  Up rose the Fathers all;
In haste they girded up their gowns,
  And hied them to the wall.    145

They held a council, standing
  Before the River-gate;
Short time was there, ye well may guess,
  For musing or debate.
Out spake the Consul roundly:    150
  "The bridge must straight go down;
For, since Janiculum is lost,
  Naught else can save the town."
      *   *   *

But the Consul's brow was sad,
  And the Consul's speech was low,    210
And darkly looked he at the wall,
  And darkly at the foe;
"Their van will be upon us
  Before the bridge goes down;
And if they once may win the bridge,    215
  What hope to save the town?"

Then out spake brave Horatius,
  The Captain of the gate:
"To every man upon this earth
  Death cometh soon or late.    220
And how can man die better
  Than facing fearful odds
For the ashes of his fathers
  And the temples of his gods,
      *   *   *

"Hew down the bridge, Sir Consul,
  With all the speed ye may;
I, with two more to help me,    235
  Will hold the foe in play.
In yon strait path a thousand
  May well be stopped by three:
Now who will stand on either hand,
  And keep the bridge with me?"    240

Then out spake Spurius Lartius,—
  A Ramnian proud was he:
"Lo, I will stand at thy right hand,
  And keep the bridge with thee."
And out spake strong Herminius,—    245
  Of Titian blood was he:
"I will abide on thy left side,
  And keep the bridge with thee."

"Horatius," quoth the Consul,
  "As thou sayest so let it be,"    250
And straight against that great array
  Went forth the dauntless three.

For Romans in Rome's quarrel
  Spared neither land nor gold,
Nor son nor wife, nor limb nor life,    255
  In the brave days of old.
      *   *   *

Now while the three were tightening
  Their harness on their backs,
The Consul was the foremost man    275
  To take in hand an axe;
And fathers, mixed with commons,
  Seized hatchet, bar, and crow,
And smote upon the planks above,
  And loosed the props below.    280

Meanwhile the Tuscan army,
  Right glorious to behold,
Came flashing back the noonday light,
Rank behind rank, like surges bright
  Of a broad sea of gold.    285
Four hundred trumpets sounded
  A peal of warlike glee,
As that great host with measured tread,
And spears advanced, and ensigns spread,
Rolled slowly toward the bridge's head,    290
  Where stood the dauntless three.
      *   *   *

Yet one man for one moment
  Strode out before the crowd;
Well known was he to all the three,
  And they gave him greeting loud:    430
"Now welcome, welcome, Sextus!
  Now welcome to thy home!
Why dost thou stay, and turn away?
  Here lies the road to Rome."

Thrice looked he at the city;    435
  Thrice looked he at the dead:
And thrice came on in fury,
  And thrice turned back in dread;
And, white with fear and hatred,

Scowled at the narrow way                                        440
Where, wallowing in a pool of blood,
  The bravest Tuscans lay.

But meanwhile axe and lever
  Have manfully been plied:
And now the bridge hangs tottering          445
  Above the boiling tide.
"Come back, come back, Horatius!"
  Loud cried the Fathers all,—
"Back, Lartius! back, Herminius!
  Back, ere the ruin fall!"                                    450

Back darted Spurius Lartius,—
  Herminius darted back;
And, as they passed, beneath their feet
  They felt the timbers crack.
But when they turned their faces,          455
  And on the farther shore
Saw brave Horatius stand alone,
  They would have crossed once more;

But with a crash like thunder
  Fell every loosened beam,                                   460
And, like a dam, the mighty wreck
  Lay right athwart the stream;
And a long shout of triumph
  Rose from the walls of Rome,
As to the highest turret-tops                   465
  Was splashed the yellow foam.

And like a horse unbroken,
  When first he feels the rein,
The furious river struggled hard,
  And tossed his tawny mane,                          470
And burst the curb, and bounded,
  Rejoicing to be free;
And whirling down, in fierce career,
Battlement and plank and pier,
  Rushed headlong to the sea.                          475
Alone stood brave Horatius,
  But constant still in mind,—
Thrice thirty thousand foes before,

And the broad flood behind.
"Down with him!" cried false Sextus,          480
  With a smile on his pale face;
"Now yield thee," cried Lars Porsena,
  "Now yield thee to our grace!"

Round turned he, as not deigning
  Those craven ranks to see;                               485
Naught spake he to Lars Porsena,
  To Sextus naught spake he;
But he saw on Palatinus
  The white porch of his home;
And he spake to the noble river                 490
  That rolls by the towers of Rome:

"O Tiber! Father Tiber!
  To whom the Romans pray,
A Roman's life, a Roman's arms,
  Take thou in charge this day!"                   495
So he spake, and, speaking, sheathed
  The good sword by his side,
And, with his harness on his back,
  Plunged headlong in the tide.

No sound of joy or sorrow                              500
  Was heard from either bank,
But friends and foes in dumb surprise,
With parted lips and straining eyes,
  Stood gazing where he sank;
And when above the surges                         505
  They saw his crest appear,
All Rome sent forth a rapturous cry,
And even the ranks of Tuscany
  Could scarce forbear to cheer.

But fiercely ran the current,                         510
  Swollen high by months of rain;
And fast his blood was flowing,
  And he was sore in pain,
And heavy with his armor,
  And spent with changing blows;               515
And oft they thought him sinking,
  But still again he rose.

Never, I ween[2], did swimmer.
  In such an evil case,
Struggle through such a raging flood          520
  Safe to the landing-place;
But his limbs were borne up bravely
  By the brave heart within,
And our good Father Tiber
  Bare bravely up his chin.                              525

"Curse on him!" quoth false Sextus,—
  "Will not the villain drown?
But for this stay, ere close of day
  We should have sacked the town!"
"Heaven help him!" quoth Lars Porsena,    530
  "And bring him safe to shore;
For such a gallant feat of arms
  Was never seen before."

And now he feels the bottom;
  Now on dry earth he stands;                       535
Now round him throng the Fathers
  To press his gory hands;
And now, with shouts and clapping,
  And noise of weeping loud,
He enters through the River-gate,              540
  Borne by the joyous crowd.
            *      *      *
When the goodman mends his armor,
  And trims his helmet's plume;
When the goodwife's shuttle merrily
  Goes flashing through the loom;               585
With weeping and with laughter
  Still is the story told,
How well Horatius kept the bridge
  In the brave days of old.

_____

[1] "Wis," an archaic term meaning "know."
[2] "Ween," an archaic term meaning "imagine."

[Bliss Carman, et al., eds. *The World's Best Poetry*,
Volume VII, Descriptive: Narrative, 1904.
From http://www.bartleby.com/360/7/158.html]

# We Thank Thee

**Traditionally Attributed to Ralph Waldo Emerson**

For this new morning with its light;
For rest and shelter of the night,
For health and food and love and friends
For everything Thy goodness sends
We thank Thee, Heavenly Father.

For flowers that bloom about our feet,
For tender grass so fresh and sweet,
For song of bird and hum of bee,
For all things fair we hear or see,
We thank Thee, Heavenly Father.

For blue of stream and blue of sky;
For pleasant shade of branches high,
For fragrant air and cooling breeze;
For beauty of the blooming trees,
We thank Thee, Heavenly Father.

[*The Educational Review*, Teacher's Magazine, Volume 24, May/June, 1910-11.]

# Part Three
## Sailing On

 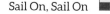

# Life Story*

## LeRoy T. Carlson, TDS Founder

### May 15, 1916 – May 23, 2016

LeRoy T. ("Roy") Carlson, founder and longtime chairman of Telephone and Data Systems, Inc. [NYSE: TDS; www.tdsinc.com], passed away on Monday, May 23, 2016, in Evanston, Illinois, at the age of 100. His accomplishments were significant to U.S. society, which he aspired to serve from an early age. Roy was a visionary entrepreneur and an ardent supporter of education.

Roy is survived by his wife, Margaret; children, LeRoy T. ("Ted") Carlson, Jr., Prudence Carlson, Walter Carlson, and Letitia Carlson; ten grandchildren; his sister, Florence Wertz; and many nieces, nephews, and cousins.

Roy was born in Chicago on May 15, 1916, to Axel and Gerda (Swanson) Carlson, both young immigrants from Sweden. The middle of three children (older brother, Vincent, and younger sister, Florence), he spent his early years as part of a closely knit Swedish community on Chicago's South Side. His father, Axel, was a carpenter and contractor who lost work during the Great Depression. Industrious at an early age, Roy helped support his family during the Depression by selling fruit and vegetables from a cart he pulled through Chicago's streets and alleys, and by working at other part-time jobs. His mother, Gerda, was a deeply religious person and Sunday school teacher. When Roy was confirmed at St. Matthew Lutheran Church, through the minister's laying on of hands, he experienced a strong metanoia (conversion experience). Believing that he had been saved freed him to act boldly for what he thought was right.

After graduating from Tilden Technical High School with honors, and after finishing junior college while living at home, Roy applied to and was accepted by the University of Chicago. He was given a scholarship and commuted from home in a car pool with good friends.

He was part of a select group of students who were test cases for an early version of Robert Hutchins' and Mortimer Adler's "great books" courses.

To quote from the University of Chicago's website: "Hutchins focused on the highest abstraction—morals, values, the intellect...and above all the study of metaphysics."

In writing a major paper for the "great books" course, Roy locked himself in his room at home and alternated working four hours and sleeping four hours, until the paper was done. His mother was chagrined because he wasn't doing his household chores, but she didn't interrupt his work.

He attributed to Hutchins and to the University of Chicago his own love of learning the meaning of new words, and his own method of reasoning, of always starting with considering the universe (universal) before going to and thinking about the particular.

He earned a BA in Business from the University of Chicago in 1938, which he mostly paid for by working in various part-time sales jobs. Roy received his MBA from Harvard Business School in 1941, supporting himself by organizing and running a successful laundry pickup and delivery service for other students.

Roy considered his most meaningful single accomplishment to be the long, book-length manual he wrote with two fellow students in the MBA program at Harvard Business School, and what subsequently happened with the manual. The three students were close friends and were dedicated to doing something important to help the United States address what seemed to be an inevitable war. The manual they wrote was on how to best organize domestic United States resources in order for the country to prepare for the coming war. It was sent to Henry Cabot Lodge, who in turn sent it to an even closer Roosevelt advisor, who in turn arranged a meeting for the three students to present it to Eleanor Roosevelt, which they did. The United States entered World War II in December 1941.

Roy served his country with distinction during WWII. He served in the U.S. Army Ordnance Department from 1941 to 1943, leaving the United States in 1942 for stations in Accra, Gold Coast (now Ghana), and Cairo, Egypt. In January 1943, Roy went to Iran with the Persian Gulf Service Command as part of the Ordnance's Iran mission to secure supply lines to Russia. Roy was stationed at a truck assembly plant in Andimeshk, in western Iran, supplying large trucks to the Russian front. These truck assembly plants were operated by General Motors Overseas Operations until July 1, 1943, at which point they were taken over by Ordnance-run companies, utilizing native labor. Roy arrived in India in August of 1943, staying in that country to work as the assistant treasurer for the General Motors plant in Calcutta (now Kolkata), where he would stay until October 1944. He served in the U.S. Navy from 1945 to 1946.

In 1945, he married Margaret Deffenbaugh, whose wise counsel and unflagging support contributed greatly to Roy's business and personal success through the years. Roy and Margaret celebrated their 71st wedding anniversary in January 2016.

Following WWII, Roy developed his business skills over the next several years through a variety of managerial positions, including working for Joseph P. Kennedy at the Chicago Merchandise Mart and for the Acme Steel Company. Roy was then ready to run and own a business, acquiring the Suttle Equipment Company in Lawrenceville, Illinois, in 1949. Suttle's business consisted of supplying standard printed forms, wire and cable insulators, and other equipment to independent telephone companies. Through managing Suttle, Roy became very interested in the operating characteristics of the rural independent telephone industry. With his entrepreneurial mind-set and negotiating skills, he and a partner acquired a significant number of rural telephone companies in the 1950s and early 1960s, which formed Telephones, Inc. After Telephones, Inc., was acquired in 1964 by a larger independent telephone company, Roy worked briefly as a business broker in the cable TV and independent telephone company industries.

Roy returned full-time to the telephone operating business in 1967. In that year and in 1968, he and a close friend acquired ten rural Wisconsin telephone companies, which formed the foundation of TDS and was incorporated on January 1, 1969. Under Roy's vigorous and visionary leadership, TDS became a leading telecommunications company, with six million customers, 10,400 employees/associates, and revenues of over $5 billion for 2016, the year he passed away. At that time, its subsidiaries included U.S. Cellular, TDS Telecom, OneNeck IT Solutions, Bend Broadband and Suttle-Straus. The Company's success has been based on the basic concepts upon which Roy founded the Company: outstanding technical and customer care services to the Company's customers, new services and products, growth through acquisitions, excellent people, and fiscal soundness. LeRoy T. ("Ted") Carlson, Jr., became TDS president and CEO in 1986, succeeding Roy at the helm.

Particularly notable among Roy's achievements as TDS chairman was his foundational role in the establishment (in 1983) and development of U.S. Cellular. His early recognition of the immense potential of cellular telephony, and his aggressive acquisition and trading of cellular licenses, enabled U.S. Cellular to become a major player in the industry.

After stepping aside as TDS chairman in 2002 in favor of his son, Walter Carlson, Roy continued to contribute to the company's success—providing inspiration, counsel, and support as TDS chairman emeritus, as U.S. Cellular director, and as a member of TDS's senior management team.

Besides being a visionary entrepreneur, driven leader, and strong family man, Roy was an inspiring force in the lives of many people. In particular, he was passionate about the value of education in bettering people's lives, and about it being a cornerstone of TDS's progress. He championed a generous and widespread program of continuing education by instituting financial aid policies for employees/associates taking college and graduate-level business-related courses, and by fostering a culture at TDS of continuous learning and personal development.

His philanthropic endeavors were focused on education. He and his wife generously supported institutions of higher learning. They funded professorships at the University of Chicago, Wellesley College, Yale University, the Lutheran School of Theology at Chicago, and Augustana College, and they funded a fellowship at Harvard Business School.

Roy's goal was to provide a lifetime of service to society. The communications industry, which meets fundamental human needs to communicate, offered the right opportunity for him to be of service. Roy's work over his many years earned him numerous awards, including Junior Achievement's Chicago Business Hall of Fame Award, Wireless History Foundation's Hall of Fame Award, the Independent Telecommunications Pioneer Association's Hall of Fame Award, the Wisconsin State Telecommunications Association's Lifetime Achievement Award, and KPMG's Illinois High-Tech Award.

Roy's remarkable spirit of service will live on through the lives of many family members, employees/associates, and friends whom he inspired to develop their own potential. Roy encouraged everyone to "never give up" in building for the future.

[*Roy Carlson's life story appeared in slightly different form as his "Obituary" in newspapers and in the program booklet for his Memorial Service on July 16, 2016.]

# Celebrating A Life

TDS Chicago celebrates Roy's birthdays over the years, and Bill DeCarlo plants TDS's flag at the summit of Mt. Kilimanjaro in Africa, all to Roy's delight.

"Care
for your
**FAMILY**."

"Find someone to **RUN** with (have a lifetime partner)."

Top: Margaret Carlson with grandchildren, June 2016. Bottom: Roy and Margaret's Wedding, January 1945; Roy and Margaret Skype-in to TDS Chicago office, May 2012.

Amanda and Walter Carlson demonstrate the "Carlson Wave" at the Memorial Service held in Roy's honor, July 2016, Union League Club of Chicago.

# Closing Remarks As We Sail On

"Sail On, Sail On" provides many stimulating insights into Roy Carlson's character and exceptional personal attributes. They were instrumental in his notable accomplishments as the founder and builder of TDS, and shaped his rich personal life. While Roy was blessed with many impressive qualities, it is important to note that he worked diligently throughout his lifetime to enhance them as he focused on serving his company and its employees and associates, his family and friends, and society.

Foremost among the reasons Roy was so successful was his abiding interest in and concern for TDS employees and associates, and their well-being. His intense focus on, and commitment to, building TDS into a prominent telecommunications company, was never at their expense. Rather it was of paramount importance to Roy to always be of service. This included creating a culture of servant leadership, ensuring that outstanding communications services were provided to our customers, championing life-long learning, and modeling "team above self" by always giving the credit to others.

His inspirational leadership continued until he passed away shortly after he celebrated his 100th birthday. Those of us who knew Roy in his 90s marveled at, and were motivated by, his ongoing interest in and concern for all TDS stakeholders, and by his unabated passion for learning and self-development.

Among Roy's many outstanding accomplishments, the positive influence he had on the lives of so many people, including my own, has to be ranked near the top. I have been blessed by having had the benefit of his wisdom, encouragement and ideas for over three decades. When I first met Roy, he said I would have his full support and that if I ever needed anything to just let him know. I went home that night "on cloud nine."

So it has been a labor-of-love to be part of the team that created and produced this most well-deserved tribute to a truly remarkable leader and human being. It is a book to learn from as well as enjoy.

*Ted Herbert*

Ted Herbert

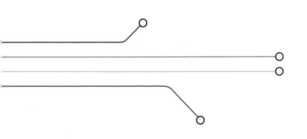